A Vessel of Furious Resolve

poems by

Cynthia Knorr

Finishing Line Press
Georgetown, Kentucky

A Vessel of Furious Resolve

For Bob

Copyright © 2019 by Cynthia Knorr
ISBN 978-1-63534-925-2 First Edition
All rights reserved under International and Pan-American Copyright Conventions. No part of this book may be reproduced in any manner whatsoever without written permission from the publisher, except in the case of brief quotations embodied in critical articles and reviews.

ACKNOWLEDGMENTS

The author thanks the following publications in which several of the poems in this collection first appeared:

Shot Glass Journal: Caught by the Roots, Out of Step
Imitation Fruit: Melancholy Vacuum Cleaner
Evening Street Review: On Verisimilitude
Healing Muse: In the Tall Grass
The Aurorean: Pasture
Adanna: Self-Portrait as the One Who Fights Back
The Café Review: The Poet Needs a Puppy, Metamorphosis
The Main Street Rag: A Little Shame Is No Bad Thing

The author would also like to thank Finishing Line Press for their creativity and expertise in bringing *A Vessel of Furious Regard* to print. Thanks to family and friends for their encouragement as well as fellow poets, including those in Barbara Bald's Bald Poets and Jimmy Pappas' Down Cellar Poets, who have made such helpful comments on my work. A special thanks to Karen Hopenwasser, who encouraged me from the start, and to my husband, whose patient support and insight have enriched both the poems and the poet.

Publisher: Leah Maines
Editor: Christen Kincaid
Cover Art: Robert T. Bennett, Jr.
Author Photo: Robert T. Bennett, Jr.
Cover Design: Leah Huete

Printed in the USA on acid-free paper.
Order online: www.finishinglinepress.com
also available on amazon.com

Author inquiries and mail orders:
Finishing Line Press
P. O. Box 1626
Georgetown, Kentucky 40324
U. S. A.

Table of Contents

Caught by the Roots 1
Things to Hide Behind 2
A Vessel of Furious Resolve 3
Broken for Good 4
Self-Preservation 5
My Own Spotted Wing Drosophila 6
Wilder 7
A Little Shame Is No Bad Thing 8
Melancholy Vacuum Cleaner 9
A Legacy of Misgiving 10
According to Gloria Steinem 11
Last Day of February 12
On Verisimilitude 13
The Spotlight 14
Ode to No 15
Last Dahlia 16
Disquiet 17
In the Tall Grass 19
Watching Ruth 20
Out of Step 21
Pasture 22
Dirty Snow on the Couch 23
The Dirty Pan 24
Metamorphosis 25
The End 26
The Poet Needs a Puppy 27
Self-Portrait as the One Who Fights Back 28

Caught by the Roots

She washed my hair in the sink
rubbing so hard I thought she'd erase me
her fingers angry wasps stinging my scalp
their venom a measure of
how much I irked her.
She swallowed her bile god knows
but better for us both
if I'd packed my bags and moved on
said sorry ma this ain't working out
you've got that awful pain inside
and I'm just stirring it up
but I was four, upside down, and
caught by the roots.

Things to Hide Behind

Bangs, as in hair over your eyes.
Bangs, as in guns.
Guns, as in what's in your pocket
now that guns are as common as dirt
in this state.
Your state, which is disheveled
and foggy due to pharmaceuticals.
Pharmaceuticals, as in Xanax
but lets not talk about me right now.
As in oxyContin,
as in procuring oxyContin
instead of enrolling for the Fall semester,
as in getting high on oxyContin
last night, possibly this morning
but not now by the haunted look of you
as you cross in front of my car.
Doors. Mine are locked
because it is dark and I am uneasy
in your neighborhood.
Yours, always locked
as if that would stop the police
from busting in.
Lies, as in you will clean yourself up
and start school in the Spring.
Lies, as in this is not my problem.
I live on a leafy street
in another world.
This is not my son.
I don't have a son.

A Vessel of Furious Resolve

Not giving up.
Throw every bit of crap at me you can find.
My idols are the women no one knows
Who fought life or death battles no one could see.
When they took their last breath, they whispered *I made it*
While an ocean of peace
Washed over them.

Broken for Good

You who prey on children,
Get woke to why no one should ever prey on children.
If you have to prey, prey on others who prey.

You who exploit children's porous borders,
Recognize that once you break those tender circuits
They are broken for good.

Self-Preservation

When her brain flooded, she found refuge
in a place furthest from the wet floor—
let's call it the brain's attic—
where she could watch the mayhem below
without sinking beneath the fetid water.
Problem was, she got stuck up there,
not permanently but she couldn't come
and go as she pleased.
The attic door locked.
And, as contaminated as it was downstairs,
she missed it. Yes, it was scary
but so was the attic with its low ceiling,
tiny windows, and silence.
When the coast was clear
(the brain's coast, not hers)
the door would pop open and down
the attic stairs the child went
with only a vague sense of being gone.

We can't blame the brain
for keeping the master key to itself.
It experienced a flood and would prefer
to stay dry in the future. Also,
it has circuits that fizzle in water
so there is self-preservation to think of.
Door open, door closed, upstairs, downstairs,
the process went on, goes on today,
even the sound of running water
can trigger it, even years after
the original flood
as if it happened yesterday
and the main characters in the drama
were still around, when in reality
most everyone is long gone,
even the dumb ass who saw the water
run over the edge of the tub
and did nothing.

My Own Spotted Wing Drosophila

What we can't see
in a bush of ripe blueberries dangling
on their stems—and I with my pail and yen
for blueberry buckle—is

the revolting squishiness of each berry
when pressed,
a transformation under the skin
that has turned the firm flesh gooey.

Thank you Spotted Wing Drosophila
for laying your eggs in my dessert,
an invasion as subtle as the voice in my ear
that whispers *you don't get dessert*

my own Spotted Wing Drosophila
invisible to the outside world,
impervious to pesticides,
a sad waste of potential

say the teachers who wonder why
the smart kid in the back row
won't grab the bright future
that dangles in front of her.

Wilder

What good does shouting do?
The damage is already done so
quiet yourself and watch
from behind the glass like at the zoo
but not the zoo. Wilder,
the glass thinner.
Peer closely at what you rarely see—
hunger so intense it splinters wood
all for some bird seed, a few lumps of suet
not much but enough
to make a return trip.
They always come back
if they've found food
and if they're real
not some jerk in a bear costume
with felt pads where the claws should be,
all the scariness sewn out of him—
although even as children we wanted to know
what was under all that padding.

A Little Shame Is No Bad Thing

So we were told
and if we weren't, we should have been,
the way it was spewed out back then—
words of rebuke that stuck to us like pollen
and shaped our modus operandi:
Avoid mistakes. Screw up anyway.
Dwell on it.
Thank god no innocent people were hurt.

Melancholy Vacuum Cleaner

It's the sound: a relentless whine
the function: sucking up lint
and the milieu: empty corridors
in the dead of night.
It's the person pushing it
stooped, sullen, underpaid
and me in my office
listening to it chew on the worn carpet
its open mouth pushing against my door.

A Legacy of Misgiving

I inherit a pink sack filled with gifts I don't want:
Tightly-wrapped secrets (hell to pay if opened)
A brittle nervous system prone to derailment
Fear of everything
Low expectations (things can *and will* get worse)
Sparkly but perilous glass shards—remnants
of something dropped.

Toward the bottom, some good things:
Silliness (sweet respite from a somber world)
Love of sports, poker, animals, although *fondness for*
may be a better term, love, as such,
having been twisted into unfamiliar shapes
with love of self so altered as to be absent.
(There is evidence of plunder here,
accompanied by a suspicious whiff of *Old Spice*.)

All in all, thanks
but no thanks.
And yet,
> when I saw her eyeglasses on the table
> where she left them on the night she died,
> I cried.

No doubt the sack she got from her mother came up short too,
and the sack her mother got, etcetera.
We are a long and ornery line of daughters, stretching back
to who knows where, who knows what went wrong
in a legacy of misgiving that won't end
until the daughters pick up their sacks and go elsewhere.

According to Gloria Steinem

The person with power takes the noun

On top of everything else they've taken
    like the law into their own hands.

They've left us with adjectives, modifiers
    they don't need because

They have rights.
    We have women's rights.
They are soldiers.
    We are gay soldiers.
They are athletes.
    We are black athletes.

We fill the ranks of best female artists in the 19th century.

Among artists of the 19th century, we are not well represented.

We've caught a few nouns of our own: nurse, rapper, model
    There must be others—

Rare fish, though, in the great lake of entitlement,
    teeming with nouns that won't bite.

Last Day of February

Spring too far away to flirt with
February sits in the corner damply
unsure of whether or not to leave the room.
Is it one of those years, February asks?
Gets no answer.

February—another word for depression.
Too short, can't spell its own name,
wishes it was May.
Now there's a flirt,
all pastel skirts and budding romance.

February remembers it has love at its center.
Helps a bit.
Maybe go out with a warm kiss?
Thinks a snowstorm for the kids may be better,
a bad one, everybody sleeps in.

All will remember fondly the blizzard of February
in the stifling heat of August.
Advantages to being a winter month
in the age of global warming.
Has not factored in the possibilities

of climate change.
February will become the new June.
It's February, people will say.
Let's get married, open the lake house,
sit on the front stoop and drink beer.

On Verisimilitude

Is there another word as delightful to say?
Verisimilitude—almost a poem in itself,
a dessert of a word with a soft center
that slips past the lips
like a cat through a crack in the cellar door.

Is there another word as generous,
offering its syllables wrapped in a bow,
a gift that can disarm a skeptic,
boost a fragile ego, impress a date.

Is there another word as dense,
packing into itself all that is true
and all that appears to be true
like so many shirts in an overstuffed suitcase.

Is there another word as slippery
twisting from v to final e like a water slide
or like the ride you took me on
when you seemed so steadfast
but were really flying by the seat of your pants.

The Spotlight

You have so big a job
shining on all those people with trumpets
where their mouths should be.
And they love you for it, preening,
dancing naked,
shooting off firearms, giving up
privacy, sanity, and their first born sons
to keep you around.

So it might come as a surprise
that some of us don't care for you.
You rarely visit but when you do,
we wilt. Like moss and ferns,
we're best in the shade.
We don't know how to suck
the air out of a room.
We are content to sit and listen

which doesn't mean we have nothing
to say: our garden speaks for itself.
We yelped for joy when the robin
we nursed back to health flew away.
We make anonymous donations.
We sing for the joy of it.
We are our own audience.

Ode to No

No, you are too negative.
Stumpy and pugnacious,
anti everything,
your *n* wants to push us into your gaping *o* hole.
You break our hearts.
We twist ourselves into Qs to avoid you.
We dream until we hear your bark,
then we make our dream smaller and smaller
until it is a single atom clinging
to the bottom of our shoe.
But there are good things—
you are flexible, sometimes meaning yes, no?
Will we ever hear a sweeter word
than when you answer *Is it cancer?*
You teach our children about hot stoves,
lead paint, the deep end of the pool.
They beat you with their tiny fists
while you give them the comfort of limits.
And there is generosity, of a sort.
You say not now, not yet, but get in the ring with me.
I'll pound you until you see the stars
that can light your way out of here.

Last Dahlia

You are the scrapper that defies the hard frost.
While most of the garden flowers hang
their heads in pale acquiescence,
you still bloom traffic signal red
saying *stop right there!* to death's
relentless creep up your stem.
I love that feisty part of you
that won't give up without a final spit:
Come and get me, you sapsucker.

As I watch you take the last sip of warmth
from an indifferent November sun,
I recognize our sameness.
Eclipsed by our bolder siblings
we discovered our voice late in the day.
We stand up when the party is winding down,
pie eaten, brandy drunk.
Few are left to hear what we have to say
but we are not leaving until we say it.

Disquiet

We are at sea and find water
in the bottom of our boat—a clue,
and the single fin approaching our fate
if we don't patch the leak
and get out of there.

Our neighbor fell from her stateroom balcony
into the ocean—on a second honeymoon.
Think of it—a millisecond in the air
then swallowed by the water, bobbing
back up, mind failing to grasp its predicament,
feet failing to find bottom,
finally a last glimpse of the huge ship
pulling away.

Does her silent husband know more than he is saying?
Those railings are neck-high and sturdy.
How well do we know him anyway?
They say anyone can kill,
even on a cruise to Hawaii, especially on a cruise to Hawaii
with expectations so high for marital bliss.

My ghoulish speculation
hides my disquiet like a moth-eaten blanket.
What I really mean is *How well do we know anyone?*
The IT guy from the office turns out to be a serial killer,
our sister's spouse has a second family in Iowa,
our college roommate racked up 100K
in on-line gambling debts.

We didn't have a clue

but there is always a clue—if we're paying attention:
a reluctance to be alone in the supply closet
with the IT guy,
an Iowa driver's license found on the bedroom floor,
the click, click, click of fingers
on the keyboard at 3am,
or something smaller:
the ghost of a bruise under an eye,
a few drops of blood in the clear blue sea.

In the Tall Grass

Five years later
the doctor told him
*You'll die of something
but it won't be cancer.*
And with those words,
he danced a little jig.
*I chased that sucker
out the door with a shotgun!*
So a year after that,
when he got the bad news
he didn't believe it
so much faith he'd put in those words
the doctor probably shouldn't have said.
But he held no grudge.
He'd had a good year
his energy never sapped
his sleep never interrupted
by thoughts of recurrences.
I sent that sucker to the moon!
Turns out, it never left the property
just found a quiet corner
slept in the tall grass
woke like a bear in spring
and danced a little jig.

Watching Ruth

Here comes Ruth the librarian, in her car
driving even now, but inching along,
peering from side to side, hands squeezing
the wheel in a plea for the fog to lift.

She passes my house and I relax,
relieved to be spared a look inside
that dusty room where the mice are loose
and books are falling from the shelves,

leaving gaps all the more ghastly
for being so random—classics left intact,
biographies decimated, some aisles clear,
other strewn with chewed pages,

one of which may have held my name.
Better our endings be swift and precise,
the drop of a sharp blade severing the neck,
or so it seems to me, cowering behind the curtain.

Maybe not for Ruth, who needs friends
more than opinions, and has turned around
at the corner—sitting tall and smiling now because
she finally recalls the way home.

Out of Step

We don't walk together
on the path around the lake—
you stop to ponder
while I press on, reaching
the same conclusion as you
but getting there first.

Pasture

We turned it into a golf course,
Pushing poetry over the rock wall,
The other side of which sits a farm
With a pasture spring and a little calf.

We will never see poetry lick
The little calf's head with its tongue.
On this side of the wall, we keep
Our heads down, emotions tethered.

Dirty Snow on the Couch

You've stayed too long on this earth
Lost your *raison d'etre*

As a metaphor, you are despair
Remember when you stood for purity?

Who would put you in their mouth now?
Let's investigate your history

You began in the troposphere—
A beautiful ice crystal attached to a speck of dirt

That word again
From whence we start, we return

How hard to jump to a loftier plane
With such heavy bags

You, dirty snow, could have fallen in a pasture
But a random gust of wind

Took you to a ditch
On the side of the highway

Was it really random, or did you *allow* the wind
To drop you there?

A ditch being where, in your heart of hearts,
You know you belong.

The Dirty Pan

He poaches his own eggs, but leaves
the pan, filled with gray, egg white-
clotted water and a scummy spoon
on the stove.

For whom he leaves it isn't important.
There are people who feel compelled
to tidy, for whom disorder begets anxiety,
and surely one of those will come along

to claim it, one more mess
to put right, borne with a mixture
of annoyance and satisfaction
akin to pulling a hangnail,

a pattern repeated so often it begs
to be broken, just this once,
to let the pan wallow, water
evaporate, egg detritus harden

into crystalline nubs of protein,
the slotted spoon pointing a finger
of blame at anyone passing
for passing.

This is not a game it will seem to say.
But it is a game, an eternal game
that the person who can tolerate
disorder longest wins.

Metamorphosis

There are too many American flags in this town
and not enough milkweed.

The flags seem to multiply—
one on a porch begets flags on other porches.
They climb utility poles, festoon car antennas.
They wave in our faces, they snap,
insisting we don't know where we are
and need reminding.

What we don't know is where the milkweed is.
Or even what it looks like.

So let this be a reminder:
It grows on the roadside and in the field.
Its stem is uniform green
with tongue-like leaves that wave in the breeze
to the monarch, whose eggs it welcomes
and larvae it feeds.

For this, milkweed doesn't ask for praise and doesn't get any.
What it gets is mowed down, sprayed, and trampled.

There are patriots on every corner in this town
but no monarch butterflies.
Let milkweed rise from the earth with fanfare.
Let flags be covered in butterflies.

The End

We think a hydrogen bomb will wipe us out
But it might be a tick
Our gaze at the sky when it should be on our ankles.

The Poet Needs a Puppy

Abusers, serial killers, adulterers, addicts,
no one is up to anything good in these poems.
The poet needs a puppy to take her mind away
from the crazed bears, the horses trapped
in a dust cloud, the black rhino rising
from an African pond to crush a tourist camp
leaving nothing behind but a broken chair and a leg bone.
What kind of tortured place is the mind
that spewed forth this chaos?
If there was a puppy, it might climb onto the keyboard
and direct the poet's fingers to sunnier places—
a picnic in the meadow, not the basement
where an innocent child is beaten, not the living room,
where mother sits on the floor and drinks whiskey
because father gambled away the living room furniture.
Maybe the poet is trapped in a failing marriage,
agoraphobic, friendless. Or was it something
that happened in the way back, the place
where memory cells keep their fodder wrapped
and resistant to retrieval but still able, like a wizard
behind a curtain, to cause mayhem in the here and now.
Whatever. The poet will write what the poet will write.
I don't have to read it. Besides which,
she already has a puppy that sits beside her as we speak,
licks her on the lips, and eats a biscuit.

Self Portrait as the One Who Fights Back

Not the one so tame she sobs with regret
when stopped for a minor traffic violation.
Here's one we'll never have to worry about
thinks the police officer.
Here's one who colors within the lines,
obeys curfew, says yes when she means no,
says whatever gets a pat on the head,
who feels the fear but not the anger
and panics like a turtle, tucked in and frozen,
making it all too easy to get picked up
and moved out of the way.

No, this poem is about the other one,
the one who isn't called on
but asks the question anyway
then won't sit down until it's answered,
who keeps talking over a pounding heart
then ducks when words like
misinformed, naïve, *hysterical*
are thrown at her,
who ignores the urge to apologize
while being sprayed, cuffed, placed
on the Watch List,
who shakes the hand of her old friend fear
and turns her panic into a poem.

Cynthia Knorr was born and raised in Jamestown, NY, in Western New York State. After earning a degree in microbiology and pursuing a career in medical communications in New York City, she relocated to New Hampshire. She discovered poetry—reading and later writing it—in mid-life, taking advantage of workshops and seminars at inspirational literary venues such as Poet's House in New York City and the annual Frost Place Conference on Poetry to find and develop her poetic voice. Her poems have appeared or are forthcoming in *Adanna, The Aurorean, Café Review, Evening Street Review, Imitation Fruit, Shot Glass Journal, Healing Muse, The Main Street Rag,* and others. She was awarded First Prize in both the New Hampshire Poetry Society's national and members' contests. Cynthia lives in Strafford, NH with her husband Robert Bennett. The chapbook *A Vessel of Furious Resolve* is her first collection of poetry.

www.ingramcontent.com/pod-product-compliance
Lightning Source LLC
LaVergne TN
LVHW041515070426
835507LV00012B/1577